Animal Migration

Animal Migration

Janet McDonnell

THE CHILD'S WORLD®, INC.

Library of Congress Cataloging-in-Publication Data
McDonnell, Janet, 1962—
Animal Migration/by Janet McDonnell.
p.   cm.
Includes index.
Summary: Examines, in question and answer format, the migration
habits of such animals as the caribou, red crab, Arctic tern, and the California gary whale.
ISBN 1-56766-402-4 (alk. paper)
1. Animal Migration—Juvenile literature. [1. Animals—Migration—Miscellanea.
2. Questions and answers.] I. Title.
QL754.M38   1997
591.56'8—dc21   96-30060
CIP
AC

Photo Credits

Art Wolfe/Tony Stone Images: 13
COMSTOCK/Art Gingert: 6
COMSTOCK/Boyd Norton: 24
COMSTOCK/Russ Kinne: 19
COMSTOCK/Townshend P. Dickinson: 2
Gene Boaz: 16, 30
George Lepp/Tony Stone Images: 9, 20
Jean-Paul Ferrero/Auscape: 15
Mark J. Thomas/DEMBINSKY PHOTO ASSOC: 29
Marilyn Kazmers–Sharksong/DEMBINSKY PHOTO ASSOC: 23
Mike Barlow/DEMBINSKY PHOTO ASSOC: cover, 10
Sharon Cummings/DEMBINSKY PHOTO ASSOC; 26

On the cover...

Front cover: A *caribou* rests in a field before its migration.
Page 2: A *Monarch butterfly* rests on a flower.

Table of Contents

Have you ever seen geese go flying by on a chilly fall day? Where are they going? Every winter the geese gather together and fly to warmer areas. But geese aren't the only animals to take such a trip. All over the world, animals are moving from one place to another. When animals go on a journey, it is called a **migration**.

This flock of geese is flying south for the winter.

Why Do Animals Migrate?

Animals migrate to stay alive. Some need to travel to a warmer place for the winter. Others need to move to find food and water. Others migrate to find a safe place to have their babies. Migration is very important. If some animals didn't migrate, they would die.

Monarch butterflies like these migrate to warmer weather every year.

Why Do Caribou Migrate?

Caribou are a type of deer that live in the far north, where it is very cold. They live on the Arctic **tundra**, a huge, flat area with no trees. In the summer, the tundra has plenty of grass for the caribou to eat. But in the winter, the snow gets deep and hard. The caribou can't dig through it to find food. The only way the caribou can find food is by migrating.

Caribou like this one migrate to find food.

Before winter comes, the caribou gather together in groups called **herds**. The herds migrate to warmer areas that have forests. In the forests, the snow doesn't get as hard as it does on the tundra. The caribou can dig down and find grasses to eat. In the spring, the herds migrate back north to the tundra.

This caribou herd is getting ready to migrate to warmer areas.

Are All Migrations Long?

Not all animals make long journeys. Some take shorter trips. *Red crabs* live on Christmas Island, in the Indian Ocean. They don't migrate to find food. Instead, they migrate to **breed**, or have babies. Every fall, the crabs crawl from the forests where they live. They migrate toward the ocean where their babies will be born.

The trip to the shore takes nine to 18 days. So many crabs migrate at one time, the ground looks like a red carpet! The people on the island keep their doors and windows shut during the migration. They also try not to drive. The crabs are everywhere!

These *red crabs* are migrating towards the ocean.

Do Animals Migrate by Flying?

Some animals migrate on land, but many others migrate in the air. In the spring and fall, many birds and insects move to different areas of the world. Many of the birds you see in your yard migrate south for the winter and north for the summer.

American robins like this one migrate south each winter.

One ocean bird, called the *arctic tern*, travels the farthest of any animal. It might travel up to 22,000 miles in one year! It flies from one end of the world to the other. It starts in the Arctic north and flies to Antarctica—and then it flies back! The arctic tern spends most of its life migrating. It migrates to find food and sunshine.

This *arctic tern* is looking for food during its migration.

Some kinds of butterflies also migrate. In the summer, *monarch butterflies* live in Canada and the United States. But in the fall, they migrate south to warmer places. Huge numbers of monarch butterflies migrate at one time. At the end of the migration, the butterflies land on trees. Sometimes thousands of butterflies land on one tree. Even more amazing, monarch butterflies land on the same trees year after year!

This tree is covered with thousands of *monarch butterflies* every year.

Do Sea Creatures Migrate?

Some animals that live in water also need to migrate. *California gray whales* spend their summers in the seas near Alaska. But as the water gets colder, the whales know it's time to move on. The whales need to migrate to warmer waters so that they can have their babies.

This *gray whale* is taking a look around the warm waters near Mexico.

Another great sea traveler is the *Pacific salmon*. These fish are born in streams and lakes in the western United States. When they are adults, they live in the ocean. But when they are ready to mate and lay eggs, they migrate back to the streams and lakes. Each salmon returns to the very same stream where it was born!

These *salmon* are migrating to the streams where they were born.

How Do Animals Find Their Way?

How do migrating animals know where to go? Scientists have many different ideas. Some think the animals remember certain trees or rivers that mark which way to turn. Others say the animals use the sun and stars to guide their way.

Many scientists think that migrating animals use **magnetite** in their heads to help them find their way. Magnetite is a lot like the magnet inside a compass. Perhaps it helps the animals know which way to go.

These monarch butterflies are resting during their long migration.

Is Migration Dangerous?

Animals migrate to stay alive, but they face many dangers along the way. Wolves often follow migrating caribou herds, eating sick and weak animals. Pacific salmon are in danger of being eaten by hungry bears. Every fall people hunt geese flying south for the winter. But even with lots of dangers, the animals must migrate.

This hungry *brown bear* is catching migrating fish for lunch

Whether it's to find warmer weather or to search for food, animals all over the world are on the move. Next spring, watch for all the migrating birds to return to your yard. How far has each one traveled? The answer might surprise you!

This robin is ready to eat a worm after its long migration.

Glossary

breed (BREED)
When animals breed, they have babies. Some animals migrate to a safe place so they can breed.

magnetite (MAG-nuh-tite)
Magnetite is something many migrating animals have in their heads. Scientists think it might act like a compass, helping the animals find their way.

migration (my-GRAY-shun)
A migration is a journey many animals undertake. They migrate to find food, a warmer place to live, or a safe place to have their babies.

herd (HURD)
A herd is a large group of animals. Caribou migrate in herds.

tundra (TUN-druh)
The tundra is a large, flat area with very cold weather and no trees. During the summer, caribou live on the Arctic tundra.

Index